# WHY ARE PEOPLE HUNGRY?

© Aladdin Books Ltd 1988

*Designed and produced by*
Aladdin Books Ltd, 70 Old Compton Street, London W1

*Editor:*        Denny Robson
*Design:*        Rob Hillier
*Illustration:*   Ron Hayward Associates
*Research:*      Cecilia Weston-Baker
*Consultant:*    Angela Grunsell

Ruth Versfeld is a teacher employed by Oxfam
to work in education.

Angela Grunsell is an advisory teacher specializing in
development education and resources for the primary
school age range.

Published in the United States in 1988 by
Gloucester Press, 387 Park Avenue South, New York, NY10016

ISBN 0 531 17082 9

Library of Congress Catalog
Card Number: 87 82886

Printed in Belgium

## "LET'S TALK ABOUT"

# WHY ARE PEOPLE HUNGRY?

## RUTH VERSFELD

**Gloucester Press**
New York · London · Toronto · Sydney

Not every child is as lucky as these children. Every year 15 million children die because of "malnutrition" — they don't get enough of the food they need.

4

# "What is hunger?"

We all know how it feels to be hungry. Our stomachs feel empty and this can make us tired and bad-tempered. Luckily for most of us we can have something to eat when we are hungry. We know when our next meal will be.

But for millions of people in the world hunger has a different meaning. Real hunger means days and days with no food, or years and years with not enough food. It means a weak body which struggles to fight off illness. Real hunger is about being very poor.

People who have real hunger can't simply eat and feel better. We need foods like cheese, beans or fish for protein to help us grow. We need fruit and vegetables for vitamins to keep us strong. And we need rice, bread or potatoes for carbohydrates which give us energy.

Without a mixture of these things people become ill. If they can't build up their bodies again slowly and carefully with the right foods, they may starve and die.

These people from Sudan could tell us about real hunger. They are poor people who have no money and their crops and animals have died during a drought. They have to wait in a food line for their next meal.

# "Who is hungry?"

There are hungry people in countries all over the world. Some countries have more hungry people than others. This may be because the country is poor. Ethiopia, India and Peru are examples of poor countries.

But there are also poor people who live in rich countries. There are people all over the world who cannot afford to buy the food that they need. In rich countries like Britain, Australia and the United States there are people who are hungry.

10

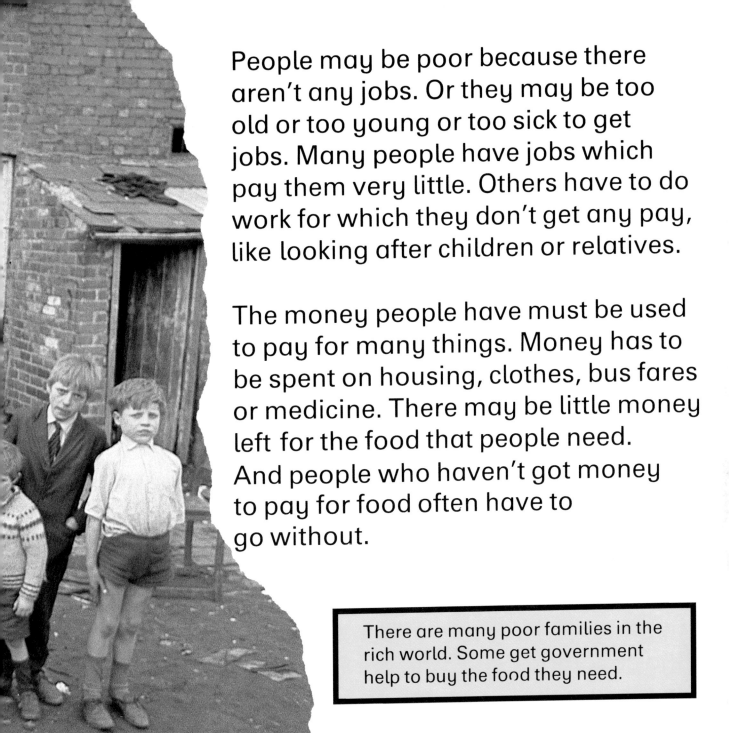

People may be poor because there aren't any jobs. Or they may be too old or too young or too sick to get jobs. Many people have jobs which pay them very little. Others have to do work for which they don't get any pay, like looking after children or relatives.

The money people have must be used to pay for many things. Money has to be spent on housing, clothes, bus fares or medicine. There may be little money left for the food that people need. And people who haven't got money to pay for food often have to go without.

There are many poor families in the rich world. Some get government help to buy the food they need.

# "Aren't there more hungry people in some areas?"

Look at the map and see where most of the really hungry people live. For many of these countries, the story of how they became poor began a long time ago. European countries took them over. These countries made them their "colonies" and used what they could produce for themselves.

Today these countries are independent. But many things have continued to keep them poor. Poor land conditions, growing numbers of people and war are some examples.

NORTH AMERICA

SOUTH AMERICA

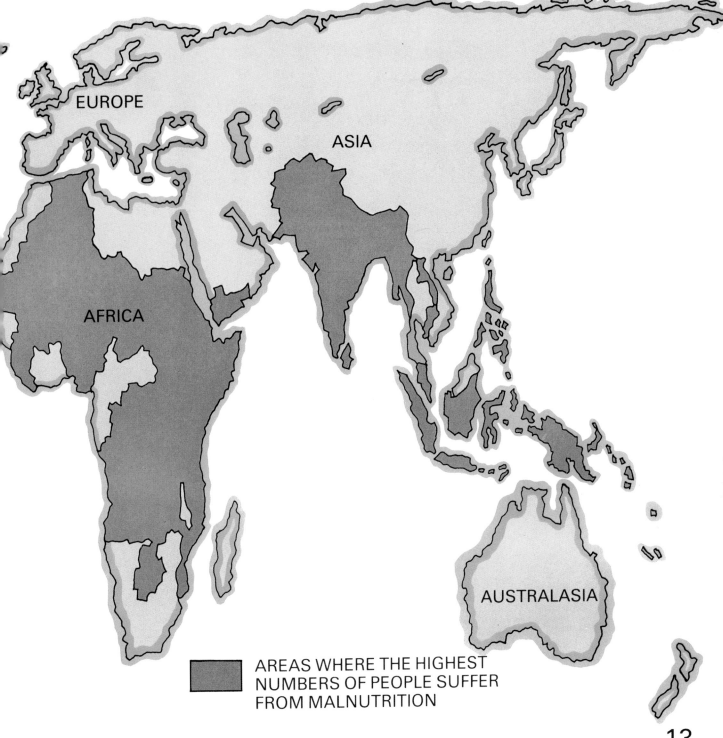

EUROPE

ASIA

AFRICA

AUSTRALASIA

AREAS WHERE THE HIGHEST
NUMBERS OF PEOPLE SUFFER
FROM MALNUTRITION

# "Why don't people grow their own food?"

Not everyone has land on which to grow food. Millions of people live in towns and cities where there isn't space to grow very much. Others may live in the country but don't own any land. These people have to buy their food. We can't all be farmers. There are other jobs that have to be done.

People like to eat a range of foods. For example, people in a cool climate want foods like peanuts or pineapples which grow in a warm climate. So countries buy different foods from each other.

There have been plagues of locusts throughout history. Swarms of locusts can eat 80,000 tons of crops each day — enough food to feed half a million people for a year.

Those of us who have land can't always grow our own food successfully because sometimes crops fail. A wet summer can mean that the wheat doesn't ripen. Pests may damage the crops. A drought leaves plants without enough water to survive and floods wash them away.

But these natural disasters are not the only reason why so many people are hungry around the world. Changes in the weather have always happened. Australia has always had droughts. Floods happen in parts of the United States and in Europe.

Poor people are left hungry because they haven't the money to buy food when their crops fail.

# "Why don't farmers grow more food for everyone?"

Some farmers grow food crops like potatoes, corn and rice. They eat these themselves and sell any extra they have. Other farmers produce things we use but don't eat, like cotton and rubber. These are sent to factories and used to make clothes and automobile tires.

Some farmers grow crops which can be eaten but we couldn't live on these things alone. Imagine eating only sugar cane or pineapples! Many crops are grown to be sold.

COTTON

One important crop which we use but can't eat is cotton. It grows on a bush. Many people wear clothes that are made of cotton.

Crops which are grown to be sold are called "cash crops." Some examples are sugar cane, tea, coffee and cocoa. Cash crops can be the only way to earn money. Farmers need money to buy more seed or tractors or animals. Countries also sell cash crops to pay for oil or the building of roads or schools.

Look at the products in your local supermarket. Many things we use and like to eat come from cash crops grown in other countries. Tea comes from India and coffee from Brazil. And the cocoa for our chocolate comes from West Africa!

There are vast tea plantations in India and Sri Lanka. Tea pickers, mostly women, work long hours for low wages.

CASH CROP

LANDOWNERS, DISTRIBUTORS AND OTHER BIG COMPANIES

PRODUCTS FOR OTHER COUNTRIES

The "middle people" in the diagram receive most of the money a cash crop produces.

The money countries receive for the cash crop will be used to pay for various things.

FOREIGN GOODS

DAMS, HOSPITALS, ROADS, ETC.

BANK LOANS AND CHARGES

ARMS AND DEFENSE

Some countries can get richer by selling their cash crops. But this isn't the case for many poor countries. Much valuable land in the poor world is used to grow cash crops instead of producing food for the people – and this continues even in times of famine.

The governments of these countries need the money cash crops bring. Many have to pay "interest charges" on bank loans made to them by the richer countries.

Poor countries receive relatively little for cash crops. By the time the crop reaches the market, it has been through the hands of companies which often take large profits. Cash crops are worth less each year, while foreign goods cost more and more.

# "Is there enough food for everyone?"

Our world and its people produce more food than we can eat. In fact many countries produce so much food they have problems selling it. If they can't get the price they want, they store the food and hope to sell it before it rots. Milk gets dumped into the sea and crops like wheat are plowed back into the soil before harvest.

Other places can't produce as much food. The problem is that some places have too much food while others don't have enough.

24

Huge fields produce large amounts of grain which have to be sold. This photograph shows a grain "mountain" – too much has been produced and there aren't enough buyers.

# "Why can't the food get around to everyone?"

Transporting food from an area which has too much to an area which has too little can be impossible. If there is too much bread it's difficult to get it to another part of the world before it goes stale. And there may not be roads to the areas where it's needed. Also airplanes are expensive and can't carry much.

But the main reason why all the world's food can't get around to everyone is always the same. Food is only sold to those who can pay for it.

This food truck is stuck in shifting sand in Sudan. Countries may have enough food even though some of their people are starving. Often there aren't roads to get it to the places where people are hungry.

# "Don't the richer countries help the poorer countries?"

Some rich countries try to help poorer countries by sending food during famines. But this can only help for a short while. Countries also send goods like tractors. But oil is expensive and tractors break down.

Linking villages with roads and railroads takes time and careful planning. But these projects help the country more in the long run. If the richer countries want to help, they will have to find out what the poorer countries really need first.

Rich countries may try to help but they often do the wrong thing. Food which a really hungry person can't digest may arrive, like this canned chicken.

29

# "What can I do?"

You could find out more about food. Write to a company whose name you see on a food package. Ask where the food is grown and how it gets to us. Tea and chocolate companies would be a good start. Or you could talk to your teachers or parents about organizing a sponsored walk. The money you raise could go to an organization which works with poor people.

And you could find out more about why people are hungry!

**Addresses for more information**

**Interfaith Hunger Appeal**
468 Park Avenue South
Suite 904A
New York, NY 10016
(212) 684 8460

**Oxfam America**
115 Broadway
Boston, MA 02116
(617) 482 1211

**Meals for Millions/Freedom From Hunger Foundation**
PO Box 2000
Davis, CA 95617
(916) 758 6200

# Glossary

**Bank loans**: Banks lend money to poorer countries so that they can build things like dams and airports.

**Cash crop**: A crop which is grown to be sold rather than eaten by the farmers themselves.

**Colony**: An area ruled by another country.

**Famine**: When people in an area who can usually feed themselves suddenly cannot. Famines can be caused by droughts, floods or even wars.

**Interest charges**: Banks expect loans to be paid back. But they also expect a bit more – the interest charge – for using this money.

**Malnutrition**: When people don't get enough food to stay healthy over a long period of time.

# Index

**Photographic Credits:**
Cover inset and pages 6-7 and 29:
Mike Goldwater/Network; page 4:
Zefa; page 9 (all): Spectrum; page
10-11: Topham; page 14 (bottom):
Tony Stone Assoc.; page 16: FAO;
page 19: Robert Harding and page
27: Oxfam.